Let's
Explore

What size is it?

SEA-TO-SEA

Mankato Collingwood London

Author's note

This book is one of a series which has been designed to encourage young readers to think about the everyday concepts that form part of their world. The text and photographs complement each other, and both elements combine to provide starting points for discussion. Although each book is complete in itself, each title links closely with others in the set, so presenting an ideal platform for learning.

I have consciously avoided "writing down" to my readers. Young children like to know the "real" words for things, and are better able to express themselves when they can use correct terms with confidence.

Young children learn from the experiences they share with adults around them. The child offers his or her ideas, which are then developed and extended through the adult. The books in this series are a means for the child and adult to share informal talk, photographs, and text, and the ideas which accompany them.

One particular element merits comment. Information books are also reading books. Like a successful storybook, an effective information book will be turned to again and again. As children develop, their appreciation of the significance of fact develops too. The young child who asks "What is a number?" may subsequently and more provocatively ask, "What is the biggest number in the world?" Thoughts take time to generate. Hopefully books like those in this series provide the momentum for this.

Henry Pluckrose

Contents

4

We measure things to find out
what size they are.
There are many different
words to describe size:
big, small, long,
short, narrow, wide.
What other words
can you think of?

These boxes are different sizes.
The red box is bigger
than the green box.
The blue box is smaller
than the green box.
Is the yellow box
bigger or smaller
than the green box?

To find out the size of things,
we need to compare them
with something else.
How big do you think
the mouse is?
How can you tell?

These pencils are different lengths.

Which pencil is the longest?

Which pencil is the shortest?

Which two pencils are the same size?

Sometimes we use a ruler to measure.
This ruler is marked with centimeters.

mms
0 1 2 3 4 5 6 7 8 9 10 11 12 13 14 15 16 17 18 19 20

Centimeters are always the same length. How many centimeters long is this caterpillar?

Jessica's height is being measured by the nurse.
The nurse measures
how tall Jessica is,
from the soles of her feet
to the top of her head.
How tall are you?

There are 12 inches in one foot.

Sometimes we measure things by their weight.

Sometimes letters are weighed before they are mailed.

Each letter is very light.

Lots of letters in the mailman's bag make it very heavy.

The ball and the balloon
are almost the same size.
Do you think they
weigh the same?

19

To find out what something
weighs, we can use scales.
We measure weight
in ounces or grams.
James is weighing the flour
on the kitchen scales.

Everything has a weight.
These scales are made
especially to weigh people.
Heavy things are
measured in pounds or
kilograms. How heavy are you?

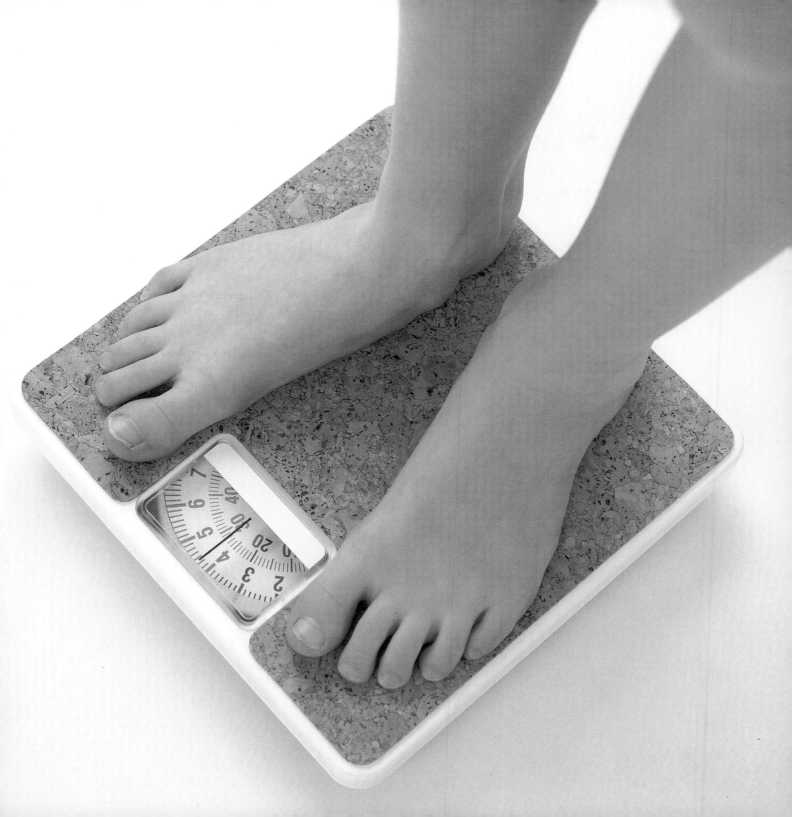

These two bottles are full of water.
We measure water and other liquids
in fluid ounces and gallons (or
milliliters and liters).
These two bottles are different in
shape, but both of the bottles
hold the same quantity of water.

This bucket can hold two and a half gallons (ten liters) of water. The amount it can hold is called its capacity. Even when the bucket is empty, it still has the same capacity.

27

Megan is going away on vacation.
Do you think the suitcase
will hold all her things?
What will she have
to leave behind?

We can measure things
in many ways.
Take this road tanker,
for example ...

We can measure its capacity.
We can measure its weight.
We can measure its length,
height, and breadth.
How many
ways can you
be measured?

Index

This edition first published in 2007 by
Sea-to-Sea Publications
1980 Lookout Drive
North Mankato
Minnesota 56003

Copyright © Sea-to-Sea Publications 2007

Printed in China

Library of Congress Cataloging-in-Publication Data

Pluckrose, Henry Arthur
    What size is it? / by Henry Pluckrose
    p. cm -- (Let's explore, math set)
    Includes index.
    ISBN-13: 978-1-59771-040-4
    1. Mensuration--Juvenile literature. 2. Size
judgment--Juvenile literature. I. Title.

QA465.P584 2006
153.7'52--dc22

                                2005056757

9 8 7 6 5 4 3 2

Published by arrangement with the Watts
Publishing Group Ltd, London

Series editor: Louise John
Series designer: Jason Anscomb
Series consultant: Peter Patilla

Picture Credits:
Steve Shott Photography pp. cover and title page, 4, 6, 11,
12/13, 19, 21, 22, 25, 27, 28, 30/31; Chris Honeywell p. 16;
Bubbles p. 15 (Frans Rombout); Image Bank p. 9 (Bob
Elsdale).
With thanks to our models:
Ashton Burns, Megan Eedle, Hattie Hundertmark,
Thaddeus Jeffries, Wilf Kimberley, Alice Snedden.